FAST JET
FIGHTERS
1948-1978

FAST JET FIGHTERS
1948-1978

MARTIN BOWMAN

 Publishing Company

Acknowledgements

Tony Aldridge; Brian Allchin; Roland H. Baker; Mike Bailey; Dick Bell; Canadian Armed Forces (CAF); Jerry Cullum; *Elliniki Aeroporia* (Hellenic Air Force); 48th TFW USAFE; General Dynamics; German Air Force (GAF); David Grimer; Grumman; Eric Haywood; Mick Jennings; Lockheed; McDonnell Douglas; Mitsubishi Heavy Industries Ltd; MoD; Northrop; Raymond L. Puffer Ph.D, Historian, Edwards (AFMC); Mike Rigg; Grp Capt Dave Roome; Roger Seybel, Grumman History Center; Royal Norwegian Air Force; South African Air Force (SAAF); Graham M. Simons; Kelvin Sloper, City of Norwich Aviation Museum; USAFE; USAF; USMC; USN.

This edition first published in 2001 by MBI Publishing Company, 729 Prospect Avenue, PO Box 1, Osceola, WI 54020-0001 USA.

© 2001 Martin Bowman

Previously published by Airlife Publishing Ltd, Shrewsbury, England.

MBI Publishing Company books are also available at discounts in bulk quantity for industrial or sales-promotional use. For details write to Special Sales Manager at Motorbooks International Wholesalers & Distributors, 729 Prospect Avenue, PO Box 1, Osceola, WI 54020-0001 USA.

Library of Congress Cataloging-in-Publication Data available

ISBN 0-7603-1094-7

Printed in Singapore

Index of Aircraft Types

Below: The Gloster Meteor first flew on 5 March 1943, and it was the only Allied jet aircraft to see operational service in World War Two. With the defeat of Germany the Meteor gave Britain a world lead in jet-powered aircraft, which was not seriously challenged by America until 1947. Meteor Marks F.1 to F.4 were all powered by the 1,700 lb thrust Rolls-Royce W.2B/23 Welland. Post-war, theMeteor F.3 served with the RAF and Auxiliary squadrons and was replaced in first-line service by the Meteor F.4 in 1948. On 7 November 1945 the Meteor F.4 established a new World Air Speed Record of 606 mph, and on 7 September 1946 this was increased to 616 mph. In total, 465 Meteor F.4s were built for the RAF, including 40 by Armstrong-Whitworth. From 1950 the Meteor F.4 began to be replaced in RAF service by the F.8. Gloster built 595 F.8s and Armstrong-Whitworth built 500. The Netherlands bought 38 new F.4s, 27 ex-RAF F.4s and 5 ex-RAF F.8s for the *Koninklijke Luchtmacht* (KLu, Royal Netherlands Air Force). NVKNV Fokker built 155 F.8s for the KLu (pictured) and 150 for the *Force Aérienne Belge* (FAé)/ *Belgische Luchtmacht (Blu)* (Belgian Air Force). (*CONAM*)

Opposite: The de Havilland Vampire prototype flew at Hatfield on 20 September 1943 powered by a 2,700 lb thrust DH Goblin 1 turbojet. Vampire F.1s entered RAF service in April 1946. The prototype F.3 flew on 4 November 1946. The F.3 differed from the F.1 in having increased fuel tankage in the wings and a redesigned tail assembly. In July 1948 six Vampire F.3s of No. 54 Squadron became the first RAF jets to fly the Atlantic when they flew from England to the USA via refuelling stops at Iceland, Greenland and Labrador. Some F.3s remained in service with the Auxiliary Air Force until as late as 1952. The FB.5 first flew on 23 June 1948 and was operated by the FEAF (Far East Air Force) against Malayan terrorists. It was also used to replace earlier marks in the UK and RAF Germany. Vampires were widely exported and built under licence in Australia, India, France, Italy and Switzerland. Pictured is FB.5 NZ5765 of the Royal New Zealand Air Force. When production ended in December 1953 (with the FB.9), 1,157 Vampires had been built. RAF Vampires were replaced by Venoms in 1954–55. (*CONAM*)

Introduction

As early as 1937, Frank (later Sir Frank) Whittle had run the first gas turbine aero engine in Britain. On 27 August 1939 the German Heinkel He 178 became the first jet aircraft to fly, and the Me 262 became the first jet aircraft to enter operational service in 1944. Britain's first operational jet fighter, the Gloster Meteor Mk I entered squadron service in July 1944. The first production Meteor Mk I was sent to the USA in February 1944 in exchange for a Bell YP-59 Airacomet as part of an Anglo-American agreement reached in mid-1943. On 7 November 1945 a Meteor F.4 of the High Speed Flight established a new World Air Speed Record of 606 mph. On 7 September 1946 Britain increased the record to 616 mph.

Britain's world lead in jet fighter design was not seriously challenged by America until 1947. In June 1947 America captured the World Air Speed Record with the Lockheed P-80R Shooting Star, by flying at a speed of 623.74 mph. Later that same year the Douglas Skystreak raised it even further, to 650.92 mph. The F-86 Sabre, America's first supersonic jet fighter, reigned supreme from 1948–53. This swept-wing fighter was one of several immediate post-war aircraft to benefit from German wartime research into jet and rocket engine development and wing design.

The first British supersonic flight was made on 9 September 1948 by John Derry in the de Havilland DH 108 during a dive. It was also the first jet aircraft in the world to exceed Mach 1 (about 760 mph at sea level). (Derry was killed on 6 September 1952 at the 13th Farnborough Airshow when his prototype DH 110 broke up in mid-air during a dive in an attempt to produce a sonic boom.) It was not until September 1953 that Britain, with the Hawker Hunter 3, recaptured the World Air Speed Record and that same month the Supermarine Swift 4 increased it to 735.70 mph. The Douglas F4D-I Skyray enjoyed a brief claim to fame when Lt-Cdr James B. Verdin USN eclipsed this record within a month with a speed of 752.94 mph. The record stood for 25 days. In October Lt-Col Frank Everest USAF set a record of 755 mph in an F-100 Super Sabre. In August 1955 Col Harold Hanes USAF set the first supersonic air speed record, also in a F-100. The FAI (Fédération Aéronautique Internationale) then ruled that the record could now be set at any altitude and not just at sea level. American fighters went on to all but dominate supersonic flight. Exceptions were the Fairey Delta, which set a new record of 1,132 mph in March 1956, and the English Electric Lightning, which entered RAF operational service in 1960.

The first of the rocket-powered research aircraft, the Bell X-1 was the first aircraft in the world to fly faster than the speed of sound, when on 14 October 1947, Captain Charles 'Chuck' Yeager USAF piloted *Glamorous Glennis*, named after his wife. Yeager ignited the four-chambered XLR-11 rocket engines after being air-launched from under the bomb bay of a B-29 at 21,000 ft. Pictured is the Bell X-1E 46-063 *Little Joe*. Joe Walker made a total of 21 flights as the X-1E project pilot, making the first flight on 12 December 1955, which was an un-powered glide. Dr. Joseph A. Walker died at the controls of his F-104N Starfighter on 8 June 1966 when he collided with the No.2 North American XB-70A Valkyrie. (*Douglas*)

US jet supremacy began with the X-experimental aircraft series. The Douglas D-558-I Skystreak was designed to investigate jet aircraft characteristics at transonic speeds, including stability, control and buffet investigations. In 1947 Skystreaks set the world's absolute speed records and these were followed by the D-558-II Skyrocket. The D-558-II was powered by a single Westinghouse turbojet and was designed to take off conventionally, fitted with two JATO rockets to boost climb. BuNo37973, one of three D-558-IIs built, is seen here making a conventional take-off from Muroc, California. It was later modified to an all-rocket version and converted for air launch. The Skyrocket first flew on 4 February 1948. In August 1951 Douglas test pilot Bill Bridgeman reached a height of 79,000 ft and achieved a top speed of Mach 1.89 during a test flight. BuNo37973 is today displayed at the Planes of Fame Museum, Chino, California. (*Douglas*)

P-80C-5-LO 47-590 *Butch* of the 45th Tactical Reconnaissance Squadron – 'Flying Polkadots' – at Misawa AFB, Japan at the time of the Korean War. The Lockheed Shooting Star saw action in Korea from 27 June 1950, first as a fighter, then as a fighter-bomber, until it was replaced by the F-86 and F-84. In 1951 70 F-80A-1s were modified to reconnaissance configuration. Altogether, 1,732 Shooting Stars were built and the F-80 was followed by no fewer than 5,641 T-33A trainer versions between 1948 and 1959. Shooting Stars finished their impressive career as QF-80 drones for missile targets and as DT-33A drone director aircraft. (*USAF*)

The straight wing North American XJF-1 flew for the first time on 27 November 1946, but the results of German wartime research into swept wings led to a 35° sweep angle being adopted for the XP-86. This aircraft made its inaugural flight on 1 October 1947 and the following spring it exceeded Mach 1, in a shallow dive, for the first time. The P-86A flew for the first time on 18 May 1948. Service deliveries began in December 1948 and the first unit to be fully equipped with the P-86A was the 1st Fighter Group at March Air Force Base, California, in March 1949. That year a TG-190 (J57) engined YF-86D broke the world speed record by flying at 671 mph. Pictured in 51st Fighter Group Korean War fighter markings is F-86A-5- NA 48-0178, the only flyable F-86A Sabre left in the world. It is in formation with F-86E 51-2849, owned by Tom Wood of Indianapolis, flying from Fort Wayne, Indiana, in 1991. 48-0178 was built at Inglewood, California, and issued to the USAF at March AFB on 18 April 1949. (*Eric Haywood*)

In July 1947 VF-17A (later VF-17) Squadron, based on USS *Saipan*, became the first operational carrier-based unit to fly pure jet fighters when it was equipped with the McDonnell FH-1 Phantom. Only 60 FH-1s were built, and they were followed by the more numerous F-2H Banshees. Ordered on 22 March 1945, the F-2H-1 single-seat fighter was similar in design and appearance to the FH-1, but was powered by the larger and more powerful 3,250 lb thrust Westinghouse J34 turbojet, had increased internal fuel capacity and a 200-gallon drop tank on each wing tip. The XF-2H-1 (BuNo99859, pictured here, was the second of three XF-2H-1 prototypes) first flew on 11 January 1947. Some 56 production F-2H-1s, ordered on 29 May 1947, were delivered between August 1948 and July 1949. F-2H-1s began service operation with VF-171 Squadron in March 1949. Pictured is F-2H-2 125052, one of 364 delivered between November 1949 and September 1952. (*CONAM*)

Right: The first unit to use the F-86A in Korea was the 4th Fighter Interceptor Wing. Sabres from this wing joined in combat with the MiG-15 for the first time on 17 December 1950, shooting down four of the enemy. However, the MiG-15 later proved to have the edge over the F-86A in climb and altitude performance. (F-86A 49-1081 is pictured.) At transonic speed in a dive the F-86 tended to nose up and if the dive continued below 25,000 ft, it would begin to roll. These shortcomings were largely eliminated in the F-86E, which introduced 'flying tail' power-operated controls and a slatted wing. North American delivered 333 F-86E fighter-bombers between March 1951 and April 1952. Canadair built 290 (CL-13) F-86E-6/Sabre Mk IIs, mostly powered by the Avro Canada Orenda engine, but 60 were powered by the General Electric J47-GE-13 turbojet and were bought by the USAF. In Korea USAF pilots reported that intermittent opening of the F-86E's wing slats caused them gun sighting problems during combat. The wing slats were deleted on the F-86F version which appeared in 1952. A new wing leading edge, extended by 9 in, was developed to improve manoeuvrability at high altitudes. (*USAF via Kelvin Sloper*)

Below: Deliveries of the F-86D all-weather collision-course interceptor fighter to the Air Defense Command commenced in March 1951. The 'Sabre Dog', as it was known, was armed with 24 2.75-in rockets. Its most significant feature was a reconfigured nose which housed a radar scanner above the engine intake. Altogether, 2,504 F-86Ds were built (53-4035 is pictured). Some were subsequently converted to F-86L standard with increased span, extended and slotted leading edges and updated electronic equipment. (*CONAM*)

The Rolls-Royce Nene-powered Supermarine Attacker F.1 was the Fleet Air Arm's first jet fighter. The prototype flew on 17 June 1947 and production contracts were placed in 1949. The first Attackers entered service with No. 800 Squadron at Ford on 22 August 1951. Some 61 Attacker F.1 and FB.1s were built, whereas 84 FB.2s were produced, the last being delivered in 1953. From 1954 Attackers were replaced in first-line service by the Supermarine Sea Hawk and de Havilland Sea Venom, although they continued to operate with the Royal Naval Volunteer Reserve (RNVR) until early in 1957. (*Charles E. Brown*)

F-2H fighter-bombers and photo-reconnaissance Banshees served in the Korean War (1951–53) with both the USN (United States Navy) and USMC (United States Marine Corps). F-2H-2s from VF-172 Squadron aboard the USS *Essex* first went into combat on 23 August 1951. Altogether, 895 'Old Banjos' were delivered to the USN and USMC between 1949 to late 1953. Included in this total are 14 F-2H-2Ns with APS-6 radar installed in the nose used as carrier-based night-fighters and 89 F-2H-2P photo-reconnaissance models. Some 25 F-2H-2s were modified to F-2H-2B standard during construction, with strengthened wings and hardpoints for bombs to carry a Mk7 or Mk 8 nuclear bomb under the port wing. The last 'Old Banjos' were withdrawn from first-line service in 1959 but some continued to operate in the Reserve until 1965. Pictured is an F-2H on approach to its carrier in the late 1950s. (*Roland H. Baker Coll*)

A Rolls-Royce 5,000 lb thrust Nene was installed in the first Grumman XF9F-2, which first flew on 24 November 1947. The XF9F-3 first flew on 16 August 1948, powered by a 4,600 lb thrust Allison J33-A-8, similar in size to the Nene. Contracts for 47 F9F-2s with the Pratt & Whitney J42-P-6 version of the Nene and 54 F9F-3s with Allison J33-A-8s followed. Since the powerplants were not inter-changeable, after October 1949 all F9F-3s were converted to F9F-2s. VF-51 was the first unit to receive the F9F Panther, when it replaced its FJ-1 Furies in May 1949. The Panthers began operations from USS *Boxer* in September. Pictured is F9F-2 BuNo122567, one of 567 F9F-2s built. (*Grumman*)

A F9F-2B Panther of VF-112 taxies in on *Philippine Sea* (CV-47) after a mission over North Korea (1950–51). The Panther was to remain the USN's first-line jet fighter throughout the first year of the Korean War, the first F9F-2s to see action being those of VF-51 aboard USS *Valley Forge*, on 3 July 1950. Of the 826 USN and USMC jets deployed, no fewer than 715 were F9F-2s, and they flew about 78,000 combat sorties. USMC Panthers flew missions from land bases. The Panther was the first Navy jet to down another jet aircraft, when Lt-Cdr William T. Amen, CAG (Civil Air Guard) of VF-111 (flying a VF-112 F9F) destroyed a MiG-15 during a raid on bridges at Sinuiju on the Valu on 9 November 1950. Some 621 F9F-2s were built, followed by 109 F9F-4s and 595 F9F-5s. The Allison A33-A-16 used on the F9F-4 was replaced by a Pratt & Whitney J48-P-2 (modelled on the Rolls-Royce Tay) on the F9F-5, which differed from previous models in having a higher pointed tail. By December 1952 619 F9F-5s had been accepted. The final production model of the Panther was the F9F-5P photo-reconnaissance version, of which 36 were built. The last Panthers, operated by VMF(AW)-314 USMC, were withdrawn from service in 1957. (*Roland H. Baker*)

The single Douglas X-3 Stiletto (49-2892), pictured here on the right with the D-558-II Skyrocket, made its first flight in October 1952. The Stiletto was built to investigate the design features of an aircraft suitable for sustained supersonic speeds. A secondary purpose of the aircraft was to test new materials such as titanium. Powered by two Westinghouse XJ-35 afterburning turbojets, the X-3 was capable of take-off and landing under its own power. It had a top speed of just over Mach 1 and reached an altitude of 41,318 ft. It is currently displayed at the USAF Museum at Wright-Patterson, Dayton, Ohio. (*Douglas*)

The Douglas F3D-2 Skyknight entered service in 1949 and saw widespread action in Korea with VMF(N)-513 USMC (pictured). On 2 November 1952 the first jet night kill was made when Major William Stratton and his radar operator M/Sgt Hans Hoagland (of VMF(N)-513) shot down a Yak-15. The F3D served with four USMC night-fighter squadrons in Korea and scored more kills over enemy aircraft than any other USN aircraft. Some 261 F3D-2s were built. A few EF-10Bs served in the Vietnam War, with Marine Composite Reconnaissance Squadron One, when they were used as ECM (Electronic Counter Measures) platforms from 10 April 1965 until 1969. The last USMC EF-10Bs were finally retired on 31 May 1970. (*Douglas*)

Lockheed F-94A Starfires entered service with the 319th All-Weather Fighter Squadron, 325th Fighter Interceptor Group, in CONAC (Continental Air Command) in June 1950. Some 109 F-94As were built, followed, from April 1951 to January 1952, by 355 improved F-94Bs. Only five Starfire squadrons operated outside the mainland US in Japan. Two of these (68th and 319th) served in Korea. (F-94B-5-LO 51-5475 is pictured in Japan.) At first the Starfires operated well behind the front line to avoid their top secret equipment falling into enemy hands, but from 1952 onwards they were used as escort fighters on night raids with B-29s. The first of four Starfire victories in Korea was made on the night of 30/31 January 1953 when a 319th F-94B flown by Capt Ben L. Fithian and his radar observer, Lt Sam R. Lyons, shot down a La-9. Some 4,694 missions were flown by Starfires. Some 279 F-94Cs powered by the more powerful Pratt & Whitney J48-P-5 (Rolls-Royce Tay) engine followed. All 853 F-94A, -B and -Cs built between December 1949 and May 1954 were used to equip CONAC (from 1951, Air Defense Command). From 1953 onwards, F-94A/B aircraft were gradually transferred to the ANG (Air National Guard). (USAF)

18

Republic F-84G-15 Thunderjet 51-1199 fighter-bomber from the 49th FBW in Japan at the time of the Korean War. The F-84G was the last unswept wing aircraft to be deployed by the USAF and was used by SAC (Strategic Air Command) until 1956, and for a few more years afterwards by TAC (Tactical Air Command). Some 3,025 F-84Gs were built, the last deliveries being made on 27 July 1953, the last day of the Korean War. In total, 3,025 F-84Gs were built, 1,936 of which served in NATO air forces. (*USAF*)

At the end of 1949 Republic began developing a swept-wing version of the F-84 Thunderjet, which was successfully achieved by using 60% of the latter's tooling and a standard F-84E fuselage. The production F-84F Thunderstreak first flew on 22 November 1952 and deliveries to TAC and SAC began in January 1954, with the 506th Strategic Fighter Wing being the first to receive the aircraft. In all, 2,474 Thunderstreak fighter-bombers were built by Republic at Farmingdale, Long Island, New York, and 237 were completed by General Motors-Fisher of Kansas City, Missouri. Some 1,301 Thunderstreaks were used by NATO air forces. Pictured is F-84 F-61 52-6644, built by Republic. In total, no fewer than 7,886 F-84E/G and F-84F Thunderstreaks and RF-84F Thunderflashes were built. (*CONAM*)

Early in 1952 Republic developed the RF-84F Thunderflash reconnaissance version of the F-84 and deliveries to SAC and TAC began in March 1954. Total production of the RF-84F reached 715, of which 386 served with NATO air forces, 108 of them operated by the *Luftwaffe*. The F-84 variants were the first combat aircraft West Germany put into service after World War Two. The RF-84F equipped two photo-reconnaissance wings, *Aufklärungsgeschwader* 51 (EA-241 pictured) and AKG-52 'Immelmann', with training by *Waffenschule* 50. They served the *Luftwaffe* from 1959 until 1965. (*CONAM*)

The first production version of the 10,000 lb thrust Rolls-Royce Avon-powered Hawker Hunter F.1 short-range interceptor made its first flight on 16 May 1953. Some 139 F.1s were built by Hawker Aircraft Co. Ltd at Kingston and Blackpool. The F.1 entered service with No. 43 Squadron at RAF Leuchars in July 1954. The F.1 was followed by 45 Armstrong-Siddeley Sapphire-powered Hunter F.2s built by Armstrong-Whitworth at Bagington, Coventry, the first flying on 14 October 1953. The first of 365 F.4s flew on 20 October 1954 and entered service with Nos 54 and 111 Squadrons in March 1955. The first of 105 Hunter F.5s built by Armstrong-Whitworth flew on 19 October 1954. Nos 1 and 34 Squadrons operated with Hunter F.5s from Nicosia, Cyprus, during the Suez campaign in 1956. (*GMS*)

Armstrong-Whitworth-built Meteor NF.14s in formation. The Meteor night-fighter was based on the day-fighter version, with a lengthened nose to accommodate radar and an additional seat for the radar navigator. The NF.11 prototype first flew on 31 May 1950 and was followed in production by 307 examples. Some 100 NF.12s, with improved radar, and 40 tropicalised NF.13s were built. The NF.14 first flew on 23 October 1953 and the 100th and final example was delivered on 31 May 1954, bringing total Meteor night-fighter production to 547. From 1956 onwards, Meteor NFs were gradually replaced in Fighter Command by the Javelin, but NF.14s remained in service in the Far East until August 1961. Meteors served the RAF for 17 years. (*RAF*)

As a matter of some urgency – the USN desperately needed to achieve performance parity with the MiG-15 in Korea – swept wings and tail were added to the standard Grumman Panther fuselage and the F9F-6 Cougar was born in 1951. The first of two prototypes flew on 20 September that year. In November 1951, VF-32 became the first fleet squadron to convert to the Cougar. Soon, F9F-6s and -7s re-equipped some 20 USN fighter squadrons. The much improved F9F-8 (BuNo14140 is pictured), with an air-refuelling probe in the nose of a longer fuselage, and with longer range, appeared in December 1953. (*Grumman*)

The de Havilland Ghost-powered prototype DH Venom first flew on 2 September 1949. During 1952–55 Venom FB.1 and FB.4 fighter-bombers equipped nine RAF squadrons in Germany, as well as nine more overseas squadrons from 1954, the last being retired in July 1962. Venom NF.2s and NF.3s equipped seven Fighter Command squadrons. The Sea Venom F(AW).20, 21 and 22 were navalised versions of the NF Venom for the Fleet Air Arm (FAA). Some 256 Sea Venoms were built for the FAA, the last being retired from first-line service in December 1960. The Venom was built under licence by Societa per Azioni Fiat in Turin, and in Switzerland, and in France by the Société Nationale de Constructions Aéronautiques du Sud-Est (SNCA). Four Sea Venom Mk20s, powered by Fiat-built Ghost 48 engines, were assembled in France by SNCA as SE Aquilon 20 prototypes (pictured), equivalent to the Sea Venom Mk 52 and first flown on February 1952. Fulfilling an order made in 1955 for the French Naval Air Service, Sud-Est built 75 Aquilon 202s, 40 single-seat Aquilon 203s and the unarmed Aquilon 204 trainer. (GMS)

The Super Sabre or 'Hun' was the first of the Century-series fighters and was the world's first operational fighter capable of supersonic performance in level flight. Some 203 F-100As and 476 F-100C fighter-bombers were built. The F-100D first flew in 1956 and 1,274 examples were built. In 1962 TAC began replacing its F-100s with F-4 Phantoms but ten F-100 wings remained in service in 1964. F-100D-NA 55-3676 of the 20th Tactical Fighter Wing (TFW) is pictured at RAF Wethersfield in 1964. Four TAC F-100D wings also operated on rotation in Vietnam from August 1964 to July 1971, where they were outstanding in the low-level attack and high cover roles. The F-100D was not without its problems, with over 500 F-100Ds being lost between mid-1956 and mid-1970. The last F-100Ds were those of the 27th TFW, which were retired in June 1972, although the ANG continued to operate the 'Hun' until 10 November 1979. (*CONAM*)

Below: Altogether, 339 Super Sabre F-100Fs were built. Pictured are F-100 F-5-NA 56-3769 and F-100D-60-NA 56-2033. (*USAF*)

Opposite: With Britain lagging far behind in supersonic design, two Fairey FD.2 Delta versions, each powered by a 10,050 lb thrust Rolls-Royce Avon RA.28 turbojet, were built. Test pilot Peter Twiss piloted FD.2 WG774 on its first flight on 6 October 1954. In August 1955 it achieved supersonic status. Twiss piloted the second FD.2 (WG777) on its first flight on 15 February 1956 and took it through the sound barrier at its first attempt. On 10 March 1956 at Chichester, Sussex, Twiss shattered the World Air Speed Record in WG774 with a mean speed of 1,132 mph at 38,000 ft, exceeding the previous record by more than 300 mph. The project was shelved in 1957, and subsequently the airframe of WG774 was modified to produce the BAC 221 research aircraft in order to flight test the delta-wing planform designed for the Concord. It flew for the first time on 1 May 1964. WG774 is now displayed at the RN Air Museum, Yeovilton, Somerset (pictured). (*Author*)

The first British aircraft capable of exceeding Mach 1 in level flight was the English Electric P.1A (WG760), designed by W.E.W. 'Teddy' Petter and powered by two 7,500 lb thrust Hawker Siddeley Sapphires. WG760, in the hands of Wg Cdr Roland P. 'Bee' Beamont, broke the sound barrier on its third flight on 11 August 1954. (*Ken Hazell*)

McDonnell received an initial production contract on 28 May 1953 for 29 F-101A Voodoos. The first F-101A was shipped to Edwards AFB, California, where Robert Little reached Mach 0.9 at 35,000 ft during the first flight, on 29 September 1954. Pictured is 53-2426, one of the first batch of F-101A-35-MCs built as single-seaters for use in the escort/strike fighter and reconnaissance roles. F-101As were equipped with the MA-7 fire-control system as well as with LABS (Low Altitude Bombing System) computers for toss release of their external 1,620 lb or 3,721 lb special store (nuclear bomb). The last F-101A was delivered on 21 November 1957. (*McDonnell*)

The Voodoo F-101B (58-0304 is pictured), which first flew on 27 March 1957, was used by Air Defense Command (ADC) from 1961 as a long-range interceptor. It differed from the F-101C in having a MG-13 radar fire-control operator behind the pilot in a lengthened cockpit. For its primary all-weather mission it was armed with two Douglas MB-1 nuclear unguided rockets in addition to the three AIM-4D Falcon AAMs (Air-to-Air Missiles) or bombs carried internally in the bomb bay. Altogether, the F-101B equipped 19 Fighter Interceptor Squadrons in ADC (January 1959–71). (*USAF*)

The Convair F-102 Delta Dagger was the world's first supersonic all-weather interceptor when it entered service with Air Defense Command in April 1956. By 1958, 875 F-102As had been completed (F-102A 56-1443 is pictured) and that same year Daggers equipped 26 Air Defense Squadrons. The F-102A served the USAF well, operating in Vietnam from 1962–69, and remained operational in Europe until 1970. (*CONAM*)

The Supermarine Scimitar F.1 (XD238 is pictured) entered FAA service in June 1958 with the first operational squadron, No. 803, being formed at Lossiemouth, Scotland. The Scimitar was the FAA's first swept-wing single-seat fighter and the first one capable of low-level attacks at supersonic speeds with tactical nuclear weapons. The aircraft also operated in the high-level interception role with Sidewinder infra-red homing air-to-air guided missiles. Alternatively, a pod containing twelve 2-in unguided rockets could be carried. A total of 76 Scimitars was built and they equipped four first-line FAA squadrons, the last (No. 804) being embarked aboard the new aircraft-carrier HMS *Hermes* in July 1960. (*RN*)

On 25 November 1958 the English Electric P.1B prototype (XA847), powered by two 11,250 lb thrust Rolls-Royce Avons, became the first British aircraft to fly at Mach 2. The Lightning became the RAF's first single-seat fighter capable of exceeding the speed of sound in level flight. Delivery began of three pre-production P.1Bs to the AFDS (Air Fighting Development Squadron) at RAF Coltishall, Norfolk, in December 1959. XG336/C, seen here with an AFDS Gloster Javelin and a Hawker Hunter, first flew on 25 August 1959. The Lightning doubled the performance of the then-best (Hunter) RAF fighter in front-line service. It was lightly armed, with only two Firestreak air-to-air infra-red guided weapons and two Aden cannon, but its ability to manoeuvre with the best and out-climb all of them gave its pilots an advantage which set them apart from others. The F-104 Starfighter eventually had the same straight-line top speeds but could never match the Lightning's rate of turn at any speed. It was not until the F-15, 15 years later, that the Lightning had any real competitor. (*RAF Coltishall*)

The Convair F-106A Delta Dart was flown for the first time from Edwards AFB on 26 December 1956. Deliveries to Air Defense Command (ADC) commenced in July 1959 and continued until 20 July 1961. The appearance of intercontinental ballistic missiles finally terminated the production run after 277 F-102As had been built (59-0057 is pictured). Delta Darts equipped eleven ADC squadrons until 1972, and as late as October 1979 six ADC squadrons were still flying F-106As. (*CONAM*)

Sabres served with the *Luftwaffe* from 1958 until 1964. In 1957 the Canadian government generously presented 75 CL-13A Sabre 5s (formerly operated by the RCAF in Europe) to the German Federal Republic. The Mk5 was used by *Waffenschule*-10 at Oldenburg for converting pilots to the Sabre 6 day-interceptor and the Fiat-built F-86k all-weather fighter (of which 88 were received). On 9 October 1958 Canadair produced the last CL-13B (F-86E) Sabre 6. Some 225 Sabre 6s were supplied to the German Federal Republic. The Sabre 6 was delivered to *Waffenschule*-50 and the majority served in the air-superiority role with three operational fighter wings (*Jagdgeschwader* 71, 72, and 73), and some with *Erprobungsstelle* 61. In 1964 JG71 *Richthofen* replaced the Sabre with the F-104G and JG72 and JG73 converted to the Fiat G.91R in the ground-attack role. In 1966, 90 ex-*Luftwaffe* Sabre 6s were delivered to Pakistan via Iran to rebuild the Pakistani Air Force after the 1965 war with India. (*CONAM*)

Right: In April 1957 63 two-seat Dart F-106B combat trainers were ordered from Convair and four aircraft were assigned to each ADC squadron. Production of the F-106B (57-2546 and 59-164 are pictured) ended in December 1960. Between September 1960 and 1963, the majority of F-106As and -Bs underwent three updating programmes and in-flight refuelling receptacles were also fitted. (*USAF*)

Below: In its first year of service with the USAF in 1958 when it equipped Air Defense Command, the Lockheed F-104A Starfighter (F-104A-10 56-755 is pictured) became the first operational interceptor capable of sustained Mach 2+ speeds. Only 153 F-104As were built. (*CONAM*)

F-104A-15-LO 56-777 and three F104A-20-LO Starfighters (56-805, 808 and 810) of the 83rd Fighter Interceptor Squadron from Hamilton AFB, San Francisco, passing the Golden Gate bridge in 1958. The 83rd FIS became operational on 20 February 1958. Out of 296 Starfighters operated by the USAF, 49 were lost and 18 pilots killed, and in 1960 the type was withdrawn from Air Defense Command. Some 24 were converted to QF-104 target drones, while three were modified to NF-104A models. The remaining F-104As were issued to the Air National Guard, although later some F-104As, fitted with the GE-19 engine, returned to first-line service. Ten F-104As were given to Pakistan and in September 1965, and again in December 1971 Pakistani Air Force F-104As fought Indian Air Force jets over the North West Frontier. (*Lockheed*)

Above: The F-105 Thunderchief, or the 'Thud', was designed as a successor to the F-84F and was the largest single-seat, single-engine combat aircraft in history. On its first flight, on 22 October 1955, the YF-105A exceeded the speed of sound. A total of 71 F-105Bs were issued to the 335th Tactical Fighter Squadron, 4th TFW, TAC (1958–59), for service trials. The F-105D all-weather fighter-bomber version first flew on 9 June 1959, and 610 were built (1960–64). The F-105D (61-100 is pictured) was distinguishable from the F-105B by its bigger nose, which housed the NASARR R-14A monopulse radar for use in both high and low-level missions and doppler navigation for night or bad weather operations. By the early 1960s the F-105D had become the primary strike-fighter with TAC and USAFE. (*CONAM*)

Left: Until the appearance of the F-14A Tomcat in 1973, the F-8U-1 (F-8A) Crusader was the 'last of the gunfighters'. It was probably the finest pure fighter of the jet age and the Navy's first aircraft capable of more than 1,000 mph. It was also the world's first variable-incidence (to eliminate an exaggerated nose-up tendency during landing) jet fighter. The prototype single-seat Chance Vought XF-8U-1 carrier-based interceptor first flew on 25 March 1955 and VF-32 'Swordsmen' was the first USN squadron to receive the F-8U-1 (F-8A) Crusader (BuNo143710 is pictured), in March 1957. A total of 318 F-8U-1s was built. These were followed by 130 F-8U-1Es and (by March 1960) 144 (F-8U-1P) photo-reconnaissance Crusaders. (*USN*)

Above: Production of the F-8U-2 air-superiority day-fighter began in January 1959, and 187 examples had been completed by September 1960. These differed from previous models in having a new engine and a fin on the rear ventral fuselage. Pictured is F-8U-2 BuNo145562 of VMF-321 of the USMC. The Marines operated 15 squadrons of Crusaders. (*CONAM*)

Right: The F-86H, which flew for the first time on 30 April 1953, was the final production version of the Sabre for the USAF. Four 20 mm cannon replaced the six machine-guns in the nose and it had increased span, length and a deeper fuselage. At Columbus, Ohio, 473 were produced by North American from January 1954 to August 1955. Pictured is F-86H-NH 53-1521 of the 138th Fighter Squadron, 174th Fighter Wing, New York ANG, which received its first Sabres in December 1957. The squadron had completed conversion from the F-94 by the summer of 1958. 'The Boys From Syracuse' did not give up its F-86Hs until late in 1970, when the squadron converted to the Cessna A-37B. (CONAM)

Hunter F.58 J-4033 on finals to Dübendorf. In Swiss Air Force service, Hunters served with nine *Fliegerstaffeln* until replaced by F-5Es, *Fliegerstaffel* 18 being the first to convert to the F-5E in January 1979. *Fliegerstaffel* 11 formed the *Patrouille de Swiss* aerobatic display team. The Hunter was the last combat aircraft to enable a Swiss militia pilot to achieve fully operational status. (*Author*)

Between July 1961 and May 1962, the RCAF received 56 F-101Bs and 10 F-101F two-seat combat-capable trainers from the USAF for the defence of North America. The Voodoos in Canadian service were redesignated CF-101Bs/CF-101Fs respectively, and they were assigned RCAF serials using the last three digits of their USAF serials. Pictured are 17392 and 17468 (USAF F-101B-115MC 59-392 and F-101B-120MC 59-468). (*GMS*)

Canadian aircrews running to their CF-101Bs during a quick reaction alert. (*GMS*)

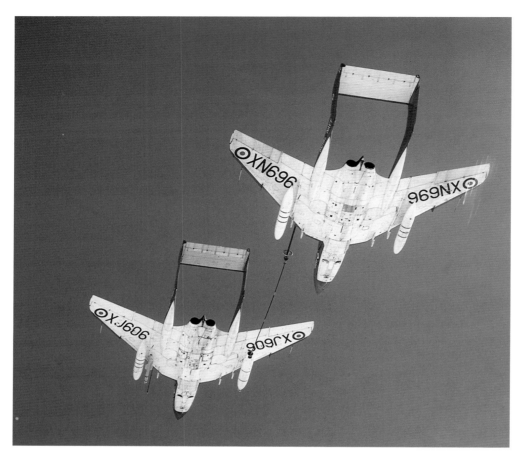

Left: De Havilland Sea Vixen FAW.1s XN696 and XJ606 are shown air-to-air refuelling in March 1964. The Sea Vixen was the Fleet Air Arm's first swept-wing two-seat all-weather fighter. The prototype first flew on 26 September 1951 and the first fully-navalised production FAW.1 flew on 20 June 1955. XJ606 was one of a batch of 29 ordered in June 1959 and XN696 was one of a final batch of 29 ordered in August 1960, which brought total Sea Vixen FAW.1 production to 114. Sea Vixen FAW.1s equipped four first-line squadrons at sea from March 1960 to 1964, when they were gradually superseded by the Hawker Siddeley Sea Vixen FAW.2. (*GMS*)

Below: The 15,500 lb thrust Bristol Siddeley Pegasus Pg 5-engined Hawker Siddeley P.1127, later named the Kestrel F(GA) Mk I, was the world's first strike and reconnaissance fighter capable of Vertical Take Off and Landing (VTOL). XP831 (pictured) was the first of two prototypes (the other was XP836). (*GMS*)

F-8U-1 (F-8A) BuNo143807 of 21 Air Wing's VF-211 'Fighting Checkmates'. When war broke out in South East Asia in 1964, F-8Es were the first aircraft to fire their guns in anger, on 2 August. The first Vietnam cruise of the 'Fighting Checkmates' was from October 1964 to May 1965 onboard the *Hancock*. On 12 June 1966 Cdr Harold L. 'Hal' Marr, CO of VF-211, became the first Crusader pilot to shoot down a MiG when he destroyed a MiG-17 with his second Sidewinder missile at an altitude of only 50 ft. By the end of 1967 USN pilots had shot down 28 North Vietnamese aircraft, 13 of these by three F-8 squadrons: VF-211 (seven kills), VF-24 and VF-162. VF-211 converted to F-8Hs (rebuilt F-8Es) for its final three war cruises, beginning in August 1969 and ending in October 1972. Crusaders claimed a total of 19 victories over MiGs between 12 June 1966 and 22 April 1972.

In April 1965 F-104C Starfighters of the 476th Tactical Fighter Squadron (TFS) arrived at Da Nang air base in South Vietnam to take part in the *Rolling Thunder* campaign against North Vietnamese lines of communication. However, Starfighters carried too small a warload and even with in-flight refuelling, had insufficient range for the majority of missions in South East Asia. Eight were lost in action and another six were destroyed in operational accidents for little return and both the F-104C and -D were soon phased out of theatre. In July 1967 the remaining F-104Cs in the USAF inventory were transferred to the ANG. (Pictured is F-104G 67-14889, which was a Messerschmitt-built 'G' used for training German pilots in the USA.) No F-104Gs were built for the USAF.

The Grumman F11F-1 (F-11A) Tiger, the Navy's first carrier-based supersonic fighter, was originally designated F9F-9 (until the sixth aircraft produced), as a Cougar variant. BuNo138604 was the first of two short-nosed flying prototypes completed in July 1954 and was used in the initial trials at the new Peconic River facility at Calverton. Although it was only powered by a non-afterburning 7,500 lb thrust Wright J65-W-7 turbojet (because the Americanised British Sapphire engine was not then available) Corwin 'Corky' Meyer almost reached Mach 1 on the first flight, on 30 July. This aircraft crashed near Peconic River on 20 October after an engine flame-out and was so badly damaged that it was not rebuilt. Fortunately, the pilot, Lt-Cdr W.H. Livingstone, survived. (*Grumman via GMS*)

Below: In April 1961 VF-33 and VF-111 were the last Fleet squadrons to operate F11F-1s. The F11F equipped the 'Blue Angels' flight demonstration team for longer than any other aircraft. From April 1957, the 'Blue Angels' operated the short-nosed F11F, and did not replace the longer-nosed version until 1969. The last Tigers in service were F11As (F11F-1) of VT-26, which retired them in mid-1987. (*CONAM*)

Opposite: Pictured in echelon formation are four Grumman F11F-1s of VF-21, one of the two Atlantic Fleet squadrons that flew Tigers (the other being VF-33). The Tiger also equipped five Pacific Fleet squadrons, production continuing until December 1958. The last of 201 F11F-1s produced was delivered on 23 January 1959. (*Grumman*)

On 24 July 1959 Canadair was awarded a contract by the Canadian government to build 200 CF-111 aircraft (basically similar to the Lockheed F-104G Starfighter), later redesignated CF-104. F-104A-15-LO 56-770 (pictured) went to the RCAF as 12700 to act as a pattern aircraft for the Canadian Starfighter. The first Canadair CF-104 was airlifted to Palmdale, California, where it was first flight-tested by Lockheed on 26 May 1961. (*via GMS*)

CF-104s 12887, 12845 and 12888 in formation. CF-104s were fitted with Canadian equipment, powered by a Canadian-built J79-OEL-7 turbojet and retained provision for the removable refuelling probe as fitted to the USAF F-104Cs and -Ds. (*via GMS*)

Production of the Hawker Sea Hawk ended with the FGA.6 in 1956. After winning a contract from Holland for Sea Hawks, on 20 February 1957 the company received an order from West Germany for 68 Mk 100 and Mk 101 versions for the recently created *Bundesmarine.* These aircraft, which were powered by a 5,400 lb thrust Rolls-Royce Nene turbojet, met a requirement for a new strike and long-range recon-naissance shipboard fighter for the *Marineflieger.* Although this service had no aircraft carriers, the ability to operate from other NATO countries' carriers was desired. Though the German Sea Hawks were land-based, they retained the folding wings of the Royal Navy's FAA Sea Hawks. (The Sea Hawk was retired from FAA service on 15 December 1960 after No. 806 Squadron returned from the Far East.) (*GMS*)

In October 1958 in West Germany the Bonn Government rejected a dozen other fighter designs in favour of the F-104G and placed an order for 66 F-104Gs on 6 February 1959. Some 916 Starfighters were eventually acquired for the Luftwaffe, 652 of them licence-built in Europe. The first F-104G, a Lockheed-built aircraft, flew on 7 June 1960. Of the 1,127 Gs built, 139 were manufactured by Lockhead for the European air forces, and a pattern aircraft for both Fiat and SABCA, while Canadair built 140. The rest were built in Europe by four groups for deliveries to Belgium, West Germany and the Netherlands, and later, by MBB for West Germany. F-104G-LO KF+134, which was built for the Luftwaffe, and was issued to *JaboG 31*, crashed on 30 July 1969. The pilot, Haptm Achim Baumgardt, ejected safely. All told, the *Luftwaffe* lost 246 F-104s and 97 pilots and crew killed. The *Marineflieger* (West German Navy), lost 46 Starfighters and 23 pilots and crew killed. *(Lockheed)*

F-104G D-8258 of the *Koninklijke
Luchtmacht* (*KLu*, Royal Netherlands Air
Force), one of 95 F/RF-104Gs built by
Fokker. Starfighters entered service with
the Dutch air force in December 1962,
with No. 306 Squadron, at Twente. The
last of the Royal Netherlands Air Force's
Starfighters were replaced by European-
built General Dynamics F-16A/Bs in
November 1984. (*Lockheed*)

Folland Aircraft built the diminutive 139 Midge lightweight fighter as a private venture, the first one flying in May 1956. The 1,640 lb thrust Armstrong Siddeley Viper 101 engine was then replaced by the 4,520 lb thrust Bristol Orpheus and the Gnat, as it was now called, entered production. In India it was called the Ajeet (Unconquerable). By early 1973 Hindustan Aerospace at Bangalore had built 213 Ajeets and the Orpheus engine under licence. Finland bought twelve Gnat 1s (pictured), three of which were fitted with a three-camera nose for fighter-reconnaissance duties. Two were supplied to Yugoslavia. The Gnat trainer was developed from the Midge in 1957 when its potential as a two-seat advanced trainer was fully realised. (*GMS*)

Northrop F-5 Freedom Fighters in formation. The uncamouflaged aircraft are F-5A-15s and F-5B two-seat trainers, whereas the camouflaged F-5s with in-flight refuelling probes are F-5A-40s. The first F-5Bs were delivered to the 4441st Combat Crew Training Squadron on 30 April 1964, followed by the first F-5As in August the same year. In October 1965 12 combat-ready F-5As were despatched to Vietnam with the 40503rd Tactical Fighter Wing for operational ser-vicetrials under the code-name Project *Skoshi Tiger* ('little' tiger). It was this tour of duty which gave the aircraft its famous nickname. Six more F-5As arrived in Vietnam to help form the 10th Fighter Command Squadron, 3rd TFW. The 18 aircraft operated from Bien Hoa until 1967, when they were given to the South Vietnamese Air Force. The 'Tiger' was eventually purchased by 20 countries and also built under licence in Canada, the Netherlands and Spain. (*via GMS*)

Left: F-100s of the USAF *Thunderbirds* aerobatic display team at RAF Coltishall, Norfolk, in the early 1960s. The team used the Super Sabres until the end of the 1969 season. (*David Grimer*)

Below: In June 1956 the USAF 'Thunderbirds' aerobatic display team traded the veteran F-84 for the F-100C. This aircraft was used for eight years (1956–64), before the display team switched to the F-105B Thunderchief. However, the Thunderchief was not suited to the air demonstrations and after only six displays in 1964, the 'Thunderbirds' adopted the F-100D. (*CONAM*)

The Northrop F-89B Scorpion interceptor-fighter was the first USAF multi-seat jet fighter capable of all-weather operation when it entered service with the 84th Fighter Interceptor Squadron (FIS) in Air Defense Command in February 1951. The first F-89Ds were delivered on 30 June 1952 and 682 examples were produced, 350 of them being modified to F-89J standard to carry two Genie MB-1 missiles with nuclear loads and four AAM Falcon missiles under the wings. When production of the Scorpion ceased in 1956, some 1,050 production examples had been built and they equipped more than 30 Fighter Interceptor Squadrons, the last being retired from the USAF in 1961 and relegated to the ANG. Pictured is F-89D 52-1956 of the Vermont ANG, which converted from F-94Bs to the F-94D in April 1958, operating them until the summer of 1965, when it re-equipped with F/TF-102As. (*Northrop*)

A line-up of No. 56 Squadron's Lightning F.1As at RAF Wattisham, Suffolk, in 1963, the year that the 'Firebirds' in their distinctive scarlet livery became the RAF's official aerobatic display team. XM989/X, the nearest aircraft, is a Lightning T.4, and it first flew on 30 August 1961. In 1966 this two-seat trainer was converted to a T.54 and delivered to the Royal Saudi Air Force as 54-650. Next in line is XM183/K, which first flew on 9 February 1961 and was finally scrapped in 1975. (*via Brian Allchin*)

Right: No. 56 'Firebirds' Squadron began practising air-to-air refuelling in 1962, in preparation for a full squadron deployment from the UK to Cyprus. The squadron started training first on USAFE F-100Fs of the 55th Tactical Fighter Squadron, 20th Tactical Fighter Wing, at RAF Wethersfield, with KB-50J tankers of the 420th Air Refuelling Squadron, before tanking from Valiants. Here, F.1As XM178/H and XM183/N, two of only 24 F.1As built, and the first Lightnings to be fitted with a production in-flight refuelling probe, close in to refuel from Vickers Valiant XD814 in January 1964. In 1965 the Valiants were scrapped following metal fatigue problems, leaving the RAF with no tanking facilities. (No. 92 Squadron's Lightnings had to 'puddle-jump' their way to Cyprus that winter.) The USAF made three KC-135s available over a six-to nine-month period for much needed in-flight refuelling

practice. Operation *Billy-Boy*, as it was called, began on 5 April 1965, with 1½ hour sorties with Nos 23 and 74 Squadron Lightnings, refuelling with 3,000 lb each sortie. The KC-135's fixed

refuelling boom, to which was attached a 7 ft flexible hose and drogue, called for a completely different receiver technique to that used on the hose and reel equipped Valiants. (*Brian Allchin*)

Left: With everything down, an F-4B of VF-92 'Silver Kings' approaches the deck of the *Enterprise* (CVAN-65) to catch the arresting wire after a sortie. Phantoms first saw action in South East Asia when F-4Bs of CVW-14 onboard *Constellation* escorted the first Navy strike on 4 August 1964. Carrier-fighters were first engaged in air-to-air combat on 9 April 1965, when F-4Bs of VF-96 'Fighting Falcons' aboard *Ranger* (CV-61) had dog-fights with MiG-17s near Hainan. One enemy jet was claimed as 'probably' destroyed but one Phantom failed to return. The 'Fighting Falcons', which along with VF-92 'Silver Kings' was disestablished in 1975, held the record for the most MiG kills during the Vietnam War. VF-96's 'Great Smoking Thunderhog' Phantoms left the fleet in 1986 and the Reserves in 1987. (*USN via GMS*)

A Canadair-built F-104G, 64-17781, of the *Elliniki Vassiliki Aerporia* (Royal Hellenic Air Force). (The first Canadair-built F-104G Starfighter flew on 30 July 1963.) Delivery of 35 F-104Gs to the Royal Hellenic Air Force began in 1965. Greece also received four TF-104Gs and, later, 19 F-104Gs and 6 TF-104Gs transferred from the United States, Spain and Germany. (*Lockheed*)

Four F-104Gs of 21° Gruppo, 53° Stormo "Gugliemo Chiarini" of the *Aeronautica Militaire Italiana* (AMI). The Italian Group, led by Fiat and including Aerfer-Macchi, Piaggio, SACA and SIAI-Marchetti, built 169 Starfighters, flying its first F-104G on 9 June 1962. The AMI received 125 of these (F/RF-104Gs) as well as 24 Lockheed-built TF-104Fs. *(Lockheed)*

683-400 (MM6501) the first Military Assistance Program (MAP) F-104G built by Lockheed and which was completed on 10 August 1962, pictured with Fiat G.91T-3 KC+101 of the Luftwaffe. This Starfighter served as the pattern aircraft for Fiat of Italy. The darkened intake lips are heating elements unique to MAP variants of the F-104G. *(Lockheed)*

The first Phantom to equip the USAF was the F-4C. Developed from the USN F-4B, it was found to outperform all USAF fighters by a wide margin. The F-4C (F-110), which first flew on 27 May 1963, was intended as an air-superiority fighter/conventional attack or nuclear strike aircraft. It differed from the naval version in having dual controls, an inertial navigation system, J79-GE-15 turbojets, boom flight refuelling and provision for a large external weapons load. It also retained the folding wing and arrestor gear of the F-4B. Some 583 F-4Cs were built. They equipped 16 of the 23 TAC wings in a variety of roles, including close-support, attack and air superiority. During the war in South East Asia, F-4C crews claimed the destruction of 42 MiGs, mainly with AIM Sidewinders and AIM-7 Sparrows. Pictured is F-4C 64-0847 of the 414th Fighter Weapons Squadron, 57th FWW, TAC, at Nellis AFB, Nevada. It was stationed there from 1 October 1971 to 1972. (*CONAM*)

Above: Deliveries of the RF-4C (60-438 is pictured) all-weather, day-night, high-low reconnaissance Phantom to USAF training squadrons began in September 1964. On 30 October 1965, nine RF-4Cs of the 16th TRS, which became operational in August 1965, were deployed on a TDY (Temporary Duty) basis to Tan Son Nhut AB, Republic of South Vietnam, by the 11th, 12th, 14th and 16th TRS from Tan Son Nhut and from Udorn RTAFB. By November 1970 the RF-4C had completely replaced the RF-101C. (*GMS*)

Opposite: Eighteen C.8 and three CE.8 Starfighters (Canadair-built F-104Gs and Lockheed TF-104Gs respectively) served with the *Ejercito del Aire* (Spanish Air Force), March 1965-May 1972. These C.8 Starfighters — 62-12733, 62-12716, 62-12715 and 62-12720 — are from 161 Escuadrón (Ala n.ì16), which operated these aircraft at Torrejón from April 1965 until 29 November 1967, when the unit was renumbered 104 Escuadrón (Independiente/Ala n.ì12). Spain joined NATO in 1982. (*Lockheed*)

Left: Hunter F(GA).9s of No. 20 Squadron on anti-infiltration patrol near Pulau Thioman, off the east coast of Malaya, in October 1965 during the height of the confrontation with Indonesia. The Hunters of No. 20 Squadron, detached to Labuan, Sabah, and Kuching, Sarawak, in Northern Borneo, carried out surveillance and Combat Air Patrols (CAP). From their main base at Tengah, Singapore, they also made rocket attacks on groups of suspected Indonesian guerillas in the swamps of Johor, on the southern end of the Malay Peninsula. The confrontation ended in 1966. (*MoD*)

Above: Altogether, 503 RF-4Cs were delivered to the USAF from May 1964 to January 1974. Some 83 of these were lost during the Vietnam War: 7 fell victim to SAMs (Surface-to-Air Missiles), 65 to AAA (Anti-Aircraft Artillery) or small arms fire; 4 being destroyed on the ground and 7 having operational accidents. In 1965 the first Phantoms were introduced to Europe when the RF-4C started to arrive at the 10th Tactical Reconnaissance Wing (TRW) at RAF Alconbury on 12 May, and the first F-4C arrived at the 81st TFW at RAF Bentwaters on 4 October. Pictured are RF-4Cs 67-433 and 443 of the 67th TRW from Bergstrom AFB, Texas, which operated the aircraft from 1972. (*USAF*)

Right: McDonnell F-4B Phantom BuNo151485 of VF-21 'Freelancers' from the USS *Midway*, dive-bombing a North Vietnamese target with 500 lb Snakeye retarded bombs. On 17 June 1965, VF-21's F-4Bs scored the first confirmed MiG-17 victories of the Vietnam War, when they attacked four NVNAF MiG-17s south of Hanoi and brought down two with radar-guided AIM-7 Sparrow missiles. Cdr Louis C. Page and his Radar Intercept Officer, Lt John C. Smith Jr, together with Lt Jack 'Dave' Batson and his back-seater, Lt-Cdr Robert B. Doremus, scored the victories and they were each awarded Silver Stars as a consequence. (GMS)

F-4B Phantom BuNo152227 of VF-114 'Aardvarks' landing aboard the USS *Kitty Hawk* during operations in the South China Sea. (*via GMS*)

The Gloster Javelin appeared in eight different marks of fighter (FAW.1–9) from 1954 to 1968, with production totalling 428, including 22 T.3 trainer versions. The last of Fighter Command's Javelin Squadrons were converted to Lightnings in October 1964. In Germany, Javelins were replaced in January 1966. Overseas, Javelins equipped two squadrons in Singapore, and No. 29 Squadron at Akrotiri, Cyprus, (pictured) until the summer of 1967. (*RAF*)

USAFE 38th TRS, 26th TRW, RF-4C 69-0350, one of a small number of RF-4C Phantoms fitted with AN/ARN-92 LORAN-D (Long Range Navigation) equipment with distinctive 'towel rack' antennae atop the fuselage. The 26th TRW operated RF-4Cs from Zweibrücken Air Base, Germany, from 31 January 1973 until 31 December 1990. (*USAF*)

On 8 June 1966 a formation led by the No.2 North American XB-70A Valkyrie, piloted by Alvin S. White, North American test pilot, and Major Carl C. Cross USAF, was flown from Edwards AFB, California. The other aircraft were a NASA F-104N Starfighter, flown by Joe Walker; a US Navy F-4B Phantom, flown by a crew from Point Magu; a YF-5A, flown by John Fritz, a General Electric test pilot; and a T-38 Talon, flown by Peter Hoag and Joe Cotton. Clay Lacey, the famous aerial photographer, was hired by General Electric to photograph the formation from a Lear Jet. The formation flew a racetrack pattern around Edwards. Suddenly Walker's F-104N pitched up and rolled to the left, towards the Valkyrie, continued up and over the XB-70A's wing, colliding with the twin vertical tails, severely damaging the right tail and tearing off the left tail. The Starfighter broke in two and exploded in a ball of flame following the collision and burned as it fell towards the Mojave desert. Walker had no time to eject and he was found dead in the cockpit still strapped to his seat. The XB-70A flew on for a few seconds then suddenly rolled off to the right and appeared to enter a spin, finally impacting in the desert 12 miles north of Barstow. White managed to eject after some initial difficulty with his escape capsule. Cross died in the aircraft cockpit. (NASA/AFMC HISTORY OFFICE)

No. 74 Squadron disbanded at Tengah on 25 August 1971. From 2 September 1971 all remaining Lightnings were flown on the 6,000-mile, 13 hrs trip to Akrotiri, Cyprus, for transfer to No. 56 Squadron. They staged through Gan and Muharraq, completing seven in-flight refuellings with Victor tankers. On 19 September 1985, XS921/M, now with No. 11 Squadron, crashed 30 miles off Flamborough Head after an uncontrolled spin. (*Mike Rigg*)

F.6 Lightnings of No. 74 Squadron, both fitted with overwing tanks or 'overburgers' for the flight from Tengah to Gan on 6 September 1971. XS897/K is flown by Flt Lt Roger Pope who is formating on XR773/F, flown by Flt Lt Dave Roome. XS897 first flew on 10 May 1966. XR773 flew for the first time on 28 February 1966. (*Dave Roome Coll*)

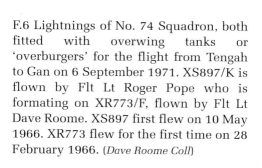

No. 892 Squadron was the first and only operational FAA Phantom unit, being commissioned on 31 March 1969. This squadron, with the distinctive 'Omega' (signifying the last 'conventional' carrier-borne FAA fighter squadron) tail insignia, embarked on HMS *Ark Royal* on 12 June 1970 after operations from the USS *Saratoga* in the Mediterranean. No. 892 Squadron's Phantoms served aboard HMS *Ark Royal* until the carrier was retired from service in 1978, the final catapult launch of an RN aircraft from an aircraft carrier being made in November 1978. The last 16 FG.1s were transferred to the RAF at the end of the year. (*RN*)

From 1968, the *Aeronautica Militaire Italiana* (AMI) began receiving the F-104S, the penultimate version of the Starfighter. Pictured is F-104S (5-41, of 5° Stormo "*Giuseppe Cenni*") the first Lockheed-modified F-104S advanced all-purpose Starfighter, which was flown in December 1966. Fiat built 246 F-104Ss for the AMI and the *Turk Hava Kuvvetleri* (THK, Turkish Air Force). In 1983, Italy decided to upgrade 153 of its F-104S models to ASA (*Aggiornamento Sistema d'Arma*, or updated weapons system) standard to enable the Starfighter to detect, track and shoot down low-level intruders. Flight trials of a modernized F-104S ASA demonstrator began in December 1984, and subsequently, 206 F-104S models were upgraded to F-104S ASA standard. World-wide Starfighter production eventually reached 2,577. Lockheed-California built 739 of these, the most widely used Mach 2 fighter aircraft ever built. (*Lockheed*)

Below: Flt Lt Tony Aldridge of No. 23 Squadron maintains close formation on take-off from RAF Leuchars, Scotland, with Lightning F.3 XP763/M in 1965.

XP763 first flew on 11 September 1964 and was issued to No. 23 Squadron on 27 October 1964. It went to No. 60 MU in July 1966 and later flew with Nos 56 and 29 Squadrons, before being struck off charge and scrapped in March 1975. (*Tony Aldridge*)

Below: The F-4E, which first flew on 30 June 1967, was a multi-role fighter designed for the close-support, inter-diction and air-superiority roles. F-4Es were armed with a 20 mm Vulcan rotary cannon and in the intercept role, could carry four or six AIM-7E plus four AIM-9D AAM missiles. Internally, these Phantoms carried an additional fuselage fuel tank, improved fire-control and target guidance systems, while leading-edge slats were retro-fitted to improve manoeuvrability. Production lasted 17 years and in that time 959 were built for the USAF. West Germany purchased 10 and others were transferred to various air forces. Deliveries to Tactical Air Command (TAC) began in October 1967 (pictured is F-4E 69-0268 of the 347th TFW, TAC, at Moody AFB, Georgia). F-4Es were sent to Vietnam in November 1968. A total of 442 F-4s (and 83 RF-4Cs) was lost in South East Asia – 33 shot down by MiGs, 30 by SAMs and 307 by AAA and small arms fire. Also, 9 were destroyed on the ground by VC action and 63 were lost in operational accidents. (*McDonnell*)

CAF CF-104 Starfighters. The nearest, 104796, is painted in 'Tiger Meet' yellow and black stripes. (*CAF*)

USAF first-line operation of the RF-84F Thunderflash and F-84F Thunderstreak ended in 1958 and 1964 respectively, and many passed into service with the ANG. Pictured is RF-84F-30 0-52-7428 of the 171st Fighter Squadron, 191st Fighter Group, Michigan ANG, which converted from F-89Cs to RF-84Fs in February 1958. Michigan gave up its Thunderflashes in February 1971 to convert to McDonnell RF-101A/Cs. Between 1956 and 1972, 13 ANG squadrons were equipped with RF-84Fs. (*CONAM*)

F-4E Phantoms 72-1479 and 72-1135 of the 335th TFS, 4th TFW, TAC, based at Seymour Johnson AFB, North Carolina. This unit operated under the control of the 8th TFW at Ubon, RTAFB, from 8 July to December 1972. (*USAF*)

The Mirage F.1 prototype first flew on 23 December 1966 and deliveries of the F.1C all-weather interceptor to the *Armée de l'Air* (French Air Force) began in 1973 to the 30th Wing at Reims. Pictured are Mirage F.1CZs of No. 3 Squadron, South African Air Force Strike Command, based at Waterkloof. The Mirage F.1CZ entered SAAF service in 1974, and was later supplemented by the Mirage F.1AZ for the air-ground role. (*SAAF*)

XT852, the first of 118 RAF McDonnell Douglas FGR.2 (F-4M) Phantoms, on its first flight from St Louis on 17 February 1967. In June 1965 the British Ministry of Defence decided to order the Rolls-Royce Spey-engined Phantom for the RAF under the designation F-4M after the cancellation of the P.1154. The first operational RAF unit to be equipped with the FGR.2 in the ground-attack and tactical reconnaissance role was No. 6 Squadron at Coningsby in May 1969. All subsequent RAF FGR.2s were deployed to RAF Germany from July 1970. (*McDonnell Douglas*)

The variable-geometry General Dynamics F-111A first flew on 21 December 1964. Originally, 50 F-111s were ordered for the RAF, but after the British cancellation, the F-111A was seen as an all-weather strike aircraft for the TAC. The first F-111As were delivered to the 448th TFS, 474th Wing, at Nellis AFB, Nevada, on 18 July 1967. Early problems in range deficiency, structure and engine power had to be overcome and in 1968, following the loss of three aircraft, the initial Combat Lancer deployment of F-111As to South East Asia was cut short. (However, F-111As performed well four years later during *Linebacker II* missions from Thailand.) Altogether, 158 F-111As were delivered by 1970. (*General Dynamics*)

Lighting F.3 XP750/H of No. 111 Squadron returning to RAF Wattisham, Suffolk, following a sortie in 1968. This aircraft first flew on 3 January 1964 and in June was issued to the AFDS. XP750 joined Treble One Squadron on 22 December 1965 and was operated by this unit until late in 1974 when No. 111 Squadron disbanded, to reform the same year as a Phantom FGR.2 squadron at RAF Coningsby. XP750 later served with Nos 23 and 5 Squadrons, and the Lightning Training Flight (LTF). It finished its days as an airfield decoy in 1987 before being scrapped. (*Dick Bell*)

In the air defence role, the 24 McDonnell Douglas FG.I Phantoms (F-4K) built for the RAF were assigned to No. 43 Squadron, the 'Fighting Cocks' (pictured) at RAF Leuchars, Scotland, in September 1969, and to No. 111 'Treble One' Squadron. With the introduction of the Jaguar ground-attack aircraft into squadron service in 1975, the strike Phantoms were gradually switched to the air defence interceptor role, where they replaced almost all Lightnings in service with Strike Command. (*MoD*)

F-4J BuNo153783 of VX-4 'The Evaluators' Air Test and Evaluation Squadron, with *Playboy* insignia on the tail. BuNo153783 first flew from St Louis on 18 March 1967 and was issued to VX-4 at Point Magu, California. Here, the Phantom was to become one of the most celebrated F-4s, known as the *Black Bunny* by virtue of an all-black scheme. The *Black Bunny* remained with VX-4 all its Navy life and retained this famous scheme for most of that time, only resorting to low-visibility grey in October 1980. *Black Bunny* was retired and sent to Davis Monthan in February 1982. After being taken out of storage in 1984, the *Black Bunny* became ZE352 in RAF service following refurbishment. It was one of 15 F-4J (UK)s acquired for the RAF in 1984, to equip a new squadron (No. 74) to replace No. 29 Squadron, equipped with FGR.2 Phantoms, which was detached to the South Atlantic following the Falklands War. (*CONAM*)

Lightning F.6A XR768/A of No. 74 'Tiger' Squadron on the line at sunset at Tengah, Singapore, in May 1968. This aircraft, which first flew on 24 November 1965, was the RAF's first F.6 and joined No. 74 Squadron on 1 August 1966. XR768 then joined No. 5 Squadron in April 1971. On 29 October 1974 XR768 was lost over the North Sea three miles off Mablethorpe after a possible double reheat fire. Flt Lt T.W. Jones abandoned the aircraft near Saltfleet, Lincolnshire, and ejected safely. (*Jimmy Jewell*)

In January 1969 seven modified F-4J Phantoms were assigned to the 'Blue Angels' flight demonstration team (pictured over California, in February that year). They made their debut at the Marine Corps Air Station in Yuma, Arizona, on 15 March 1969. For five seasons they thrilled millions worldwide with their exhibitions of precision flying. The energy crisis forced the 'Blue Angels' to change to the A-4F Skyhawk at the end of the 1973 season. (*McDonnell Douglas*)

F-8U-2NE BuNo150324 of VF-194 'Red Lightnings' from the USS *Oriskany*. The F-8U-2NE (F-8E from 1962) was the most impressive of all the Crusader versions, capable of speeds approaching Mach 2, and able to carry four AIM Sidewinders or 5,000 lb of stores in the fighter-bomber role. Some 286 F-8U-2NE/F-8Es were delivered between October 1964 and January 1965. Vought remanufac- tured 448 Crusaders to update their equipment and extend their service lives. From 1967 onwards 136 F-8Es were updated with reinforced structures and were redesignated F-8Js. VF-194, together with VF-191 and a photo detachment of VFP-63, made the last Crusader deployment at sea aboard the 'Mighty O', from September 1975 to March 1979. (*CONAM*)

Vought F-8U-2N (F-8D) Crusader BuNo148684 of VF-202 'Superheats', which was established on 1 July 1970. The F-8U-2N was a night-fighter version of the Crusader, which first flew on 16 February 1960. It had a more powerful J57 engine, new avionics, autopilot and an infra-red ray screen. Some 152 F-8U-2Ns (designated F-8D from 1962) were delivered from June 1960 to January 1962. The F-8 (and F-4) had its final sea period in USN service when reserve squadrons VF-202 and VFP-206's F-4s logged their last catapult launches and arrested landings onboard USS *America* in October 1986. (*USN*)

Lightning F.3 XP756/E of No. 29 Squadron flown by the 'boss', Wg Cdr Brian Carroll, and Victor K.1A XA933 of Marham-based No. 214 Squadron rendezvous *en route* to Cyprus on 2 March 1970. On this date No. 29 Squadron despatched five Lightnings to the island to join three others which had arrived at Akrotiri on 23 February. The Lightnings' journey from Wattisham, Suffolk, to Cyprus, saw them refuel no fewer than six times in the F.3 and ten times in the two-seat T.5 (XV329/Z), which followed on 3 March. 'T-birds' were often taken on detachment to Cyprus to familiarise new pilots with the procedures involved in performing successful target interceptions.

XP756 first flew on 22 June 1964. It suffered a bad engine fire in 1970, and was lost on 25 January 1971 when it crashed into the North Sea off Great Yarmouth after a reheat fire. Captain William 'Bill' R. Povilus USAF, who was attached to No. 29 Squadron, ejected safely and was picked up by a Jolly Green Giant from RAF Woodbridge. Povilus, who had flown 373 combat missions as a forward air controller in Vietnam, had been attached to No. 29 Squadron since 1969. (*Dick Bell*)

Lightning F.3 XP763/P of No. 29 Squadron, flown by Flt Lt Pete Hood, formating on Sqn Ldr Dick Bell's Lightning in the summer of 1970. This Lightning has just returned from Cyprus, as the panel covering the AVPIN (isopropylnitrate) starter fuel tank is still painted white. This was to reduce the temperature inside the tank, thus preventing the AVPIN from evaporating. XP763 first flew on 11 September 1964 and joined No. 29 Squadron in October 1967. It was struck off charge in March 1975 and scrapped. (*Dick Bell*)

Thunderchiefs or 'Thuds' were used throughout the Vietnam War, starting with the first *Rolling Thunder* Operation, on 2 March 1965, when 25 F-105Ds based at Korat, Thailand, attacked the Xom Bong ammunition dump 35 miles north of the DMZ (Demilitarised Zone). Some 111 aircraft were involved: 44 Thuds, 40 F-100Ds, 20 B-57Bs and 7 RF-101C Voodoos. Only moderate results were achieved and 5 aircraft, including 2 F-105s, were shot down by 'Triple A' (Anti-Aircraft Artillery). Some 60 F-105s were lost in 1965 but these tactical bombers gave a very good account of themselves from 29 June 1966 to 27 October 1967, shooting down 27 MiG-17 and MiG-21 fighters, 25 of them with 20 mm Vulcan cannon and two with Sidewinders. F-105Ds were withdrawn from South East Asia by October 1970 and in 1971 all surviving F-104Ds were transferred to the ANG. Pictured is F-105D-15 61-076 of the 457th TFS, 506th TFG (Tactical Fighter Group), AFRes, at Carswell AFB, Texas. The 506th TFG (301st TFW from 25 March 1973) operated F-105Ds from 8 July 1972 until 1982. (*CONAM*)

Line up of No. 19 Squadron Lightning F.2As. The squadron moved from RAF Leconfield to RAF Gütersloh, 80 miles from the East German border, on 23 September 1965. Here they began patrolling the air identification zone. In this role the F.2s and the F.2As of Nos. 19 and 92 Squadrons (which moved to Gelsenkirchen at the end of December 1965), were increasingly used in low-level interception. (*Brian Allchin*)

Lightning F.2A XN733/Y of No. 19 Squadron, RAF Germany, pictured in 1971. It was built as an F.2 and first flew on 1 February 1962. XN733 was issued to No. 92 Squadron on 6 June 1963 and was converted to F.2A in 1969. This aircraft was withdrawn from service in January 1977 and used as a decoy at RAF Laarbruch. (*Brian Allchin*)

Lightning F.1A XM177 in 1971 in the livery of Wattisham Target Facilities Flight (TFF). This Lightning first flew on 20 December 1960 and was issued to No. 56 Squadron on 28 February 1961. XM177 served with the OCU and then in October 1969 it began operation with various Target Facility Flights. XM177 was salvaged in January 1974 and scrapped by August that year. (*Dick Bell*)

In 1970–71 Canada's 46 surviving McDonnell CF-101B and remaining CF-101F Voodoos, obtained from the USAF in 1961–62, were exchanged for 56 refurbished ex-USAF F-101B and 10 F-101F Voodoos. These aircraft had been upgraded with infra-red sensors and other fire-control system modifications as part of Project *Bold Journey*. The CF-101Bs and CF-101Fs equipped 5 squadrons until 1983. Pictured are CF-101Bs 101026 and 10125. (*CAF*)

In the spring of 1972 BuNo148365, the third McDonnell F-4B Phantom, was converted to QF-4B drone configuration by the Naval Air Development Center (NADC) at Warminster, Pennsylvania. This QF-4B, intended as a supersonic manoeuvring target for new missile developments, was used by the Naval Missile Center (NMC, later Pacific Missile Test Center, PMTC) at NAS Point Mugu, California, and the Naval Ordnance Test Station (NOTS, later Naval Weapons Center, NWC) at NAS China Lake, California. BuNo148365 was followed by at least 44 more QF-4B drones. (*CONAM*)

Two F.2A Lightnings of No. 19 Squadron on QRA (Quick Reaction Alert) roar off the runway at Gütersloh early in 1972. For QRA in the UK, two pilots dressed in full flying kit (except for their life preservers and helmets) were always at ten-minute readiness. However, in RAF Germany, because of the close proximity to the East German border, QRA was halved. Crews spent 24 hours at a stretch on instant standby, living in accommodation just a few feet from their aircraft. No. 19 Squadron disbanded at Gütersloh on 31 December 1976 and reformed at Wildenrath on 1 January 1977 with the Phantom FGR.2. (*Brian Allchin*)

A Hawker Siddeley-built Sea Vixen FAW.2 of No. 899 Squadron being catapulted from HMS *Eagle* in 1972. The FAW.2 differed from the FAW.1 in having provision for more fuel and a launching system for Red-Top air-to-air guided missiles. The last of 29 FAW.2s was completed in 1966. In addition, a further 67 FAW.2s were conversions from the FAW.1. No. 899 Squadron was the first of four first-line FAA squadrons to receive Sea Vixen FAW.2s, from December 1963. It was the last squadron to operate them, aboard HMS *Eagle*, to the end of their service in 1972. (*Jerry Cullum*)

Over 350 Republic F-105 Thunderchiefs were lost in more than 20,000 missions in South East Asia, mainly to AAA fire. The 466th TFS, AFRes, operated the F-105B (57-839 is pictured) at Hill AFB, Utah, from 1 January 1973 until May 1981, when the unit re-equipped with F-105Ds and Fs. (*CONAM*)

Republic F-105G Wild Weasels 62-4434 of the 561st TFS, 35th TFW, which operated from George AFB, California, from 15 July 1973. Some 143 two-seat F-105F Thunderchiefs were built, the first flying on 11 June 1963. F-105G Wild Weasels were modified two-seat F-105Fs. From November 1965, 86 F-105G Wild Weasels equipped as electronic warfare platforms were used in South East Asia to neutralise the guidance system of the SAM missiles. The F-105Gs stayed in Vietnam until the end of the war. The 561st TFS was one of two F-105G squadrons which served TAC's 35th TFW until replaced by F-4Gs, on 12 July 1980. The last Thuds were phased out of service in 1984. (*CONAM*)

Beginning on 3 April 1972, the first F-106A/Bs were delivered to the ANG, when Montana's 186th FIS took delivery of its Darts. By 1974 six ANG squadrons were flying F-106s and in mid-1983, 130 Darts were still operational with ANG wings. Montana relinquished its 'Sixes' (57-2482 and 57-2490 are pictured) in 1987 in order to re-equip with F-16A/Bs. The last USAF Darts were retired from first-line service in 1988, when many began conversion to QF-106 drones. New Jersey Devils 119th FIS retired the last F-106s in ANG service on 1 August 1988. (*USAF*)

Hawker Hunter FGA.9 of No. 45 Squadron, which operated the type from August 1972 to June 1976, firing a salvo of 3-in rockets. FGA.9s were converted Mk 6 fighters, and the first of 102 of these fighter ground-attack versions flew on 3 July 1959. The last Hunter FGA.9s were finally withdrawn from first-line service at the end of 1971 and the remaining FGA.9 trainers were replaced by Hawks in 1980. (*BAe*)

USAFE F-4D 65-0699 of the 493rd TFS, 48th 'Statue of Liberty' TFW, at RAF Lakenheath, Suffolk. The 48th TFW received the remainder of its F-4D aircraft in September 1974. For two years the unit had averaged 26 Phantoms assigned, but finally reached its authorised complement of 72 during the July–September 1974 quarter. (*USAFE*)

F-4EJ 77-8394 is one of 127 F-4EJs built by Mitsubishi Jukogyo KK (Mitsubishi Heavy Industries Ltd) for the *Nihon Koku Jieitai*, or Japanese Air Self Defence Force. The F-4EJ differed from the F-4E in being optimised for the air defence role and as such dispensed with the AN/AJB-7 bombing system and the provision for carrying air-to-ground weapons. The first two McDonnell-built F-4EJs were ordered on 1 November 1968 and were followed by 11 aircraft delivered by McDonnell in kit form for assembly in Japan. (*CONAM*)

McDonnell also built 14 RF-4EJ unarmed reconnaissance versions (57-6913 pictured) for the *Nihon Koku Jieitai*. These Phantoms were delivered to Japan between November 1974 and June 1975. (*CONAM*)

General Dynamics F-111E 68-046 of the 20th TFW, TAC, at RAF Upper Heyford, Oxfordshire, England. The first F-111E flew on 20 August 1969 and 94 models were delivered, from 1969 to 28 May 1971. The 79th TFS, 20th TFW, received the first two F-111Es on 12 September 1970. The 20th TFW began transferring its F-111Es back to the USA in 1992 prior to inactivating and the closure of RAF Upper Heyford. (*Author*)

General Dynamics built 24 F-111Cs for the Royal Australian Air Force. The F-111C first flew in July 1968. The RAAF received all its F111Cs between 6 September 1968 and 26 November 1973. Pictured is F-111C 67-135. (*CONAM*)

The 48th TFW at RAF Lakenheath, Suffolk, was the last in the USAFE to convert to F-4s. The F-4s were retained until 1976, when the wing began conversion to the F-111F, the first three arriving at Lakenheath on 1 March 1976. The first 30 F-111Fs (106 were built) were delivered to the 374th TFW at Mountain Home AFB in September 1971. After serving with the 366th TFW, the F-111Fs were assigned to the 48th TFW. Pictured taking off is F-111F 73-716 of the 495th TFS, 48th TFW. (*Author*)

Between June 1973 to April 1976 the *Luftwaffe* received 175 F-4Fs manufactured from major assemblies produced by MBB and VFW-Fokker in Germany and GE J79 engines built under licence by Motoren-und-Turbinen-Union München GmbH. Pictured are 38+40 and 37+30. Under the *Peace Rhine* programme, the F-4Fs were retrofitted with in-flight refuelling receptacles and armed with Sparrow air-to-air missiles. (*GAF*)

During 1974–76, Greece received 38 F-4E Phantoms (and two additional aircraft as attrition replacements) for its *Elliniki Aeroporia*, or Hellenic Air Force. These were followed (1978–79) by a further 18 F-4E aircraft. (*HAF*)

On 13 June 1974, following the withdrawal of US aid and Greek secession from NATO, Greece signed an agreement with France for the purchase of 40 Matra 550 Magic-armed Dassault Mirage F.1CG interceptors to replace its F-102A Delta Daggers in the *Elliniki Aeroporia*, or Hellenic Air Force. On 5 August 1975 the first of these began to reach the 114 *Ptérix Mahis* (combat wing) at Tanagra. The last Mirage F.1CGs were delivered in 1977. (*HAF*)

During 1975–77, the 340 and 345 *Mire* (squadrons) *Dioseos Bombardismoy* (fighter-bomber), 115 *Ptérix Mahis*, (combat wing) replaced their ageing F-84F Thunderstreaks (F-84F 37203 is pictured) with A-7H Corsairs for maritime tactical air support. (*HAF*)

By the end of the 1970s the Hellenic Air Force still retained a number of Republic RF-84F Thunderflashes. The 348 *Mira Taktikas Anagnoriseos* (Tactical Reconnaissance Squadron), 110 *Ptérix Mahis* (Combat Wing), operated a flight of 18 RF-84Fs for daylight tactical reconnaissance, together with 12 F-84F Thunderstreaks and 7 RF-4E Phantoms in a separate flight for day-and-night all-weather tactical reconnaissance. (*HAF*)

An RAF Lightning refuels from a USAF KC-135 tanker in the summer of 1976. (*Brian Allchin*)

Nearing the end of an era – F.6 Lightnings of No. 11 Squadron during a refuelling sortie in 1976. The nearest Lightning is XS921/L, which first flew on 17 November 1966. It was lost on 19 September 1985 after an uncontrolled spin, caused by the control column being moved fully left, possibly caused by a loose article. Fortunately, the pilot ejected safely. XS921 crashed in the North Sea, 30 miles off Flamborough Head. (*Mick Jennings*)

USAFE F-4E Phantoms of the 526th TFS, 86th TFW, refuelling from KC-135A 55-3143 of the 197th Air Refuelling Squadron, 161st ARG (Air Refuelling Group), Arizona ANG, which converted from KC-97Ls in October 1977. The 86th TFW operated the F-4E from Ramstein AB, West Germany, from 31 January 1973 until July 1986. (*USAF*)

The McDonnell Douglas F-15A made its first flight on 27 July 1972. In February 1973 the company received orders, on a fly-before-buy basis, for 18 F-15As, 2 dual-seat TF-15A trainer development aircraft, and 23 F-15A and 7 TF-15A production models. The first units to receive the Eagle in the USA were the 555th (F-15A 73-0090 is pictured) and 461st Tactical Fighter Training Squadrons, 58th Tactical Fighter Training Wing, at Luke AFB, Arizona, on 14 November 1974. From January 1976, the first operational F-15As equipped the 27th TFS, 1st TFW, at Langley AFB, Virginia. (*CONAM*)

In the USAFE the F-15A Eagle first equipped the 525th TFS, 36th TFW, at Bitburg AB, West Germany, on 27 April 1977. Pictured, in October 1978, is 76-0009 of the 53rd TFS. A total of 384 F-15As was built (including 19 for Israel), followed by 61 two-seat F-15Bs (including 2 for Israel). (*CONAM*)

TF-15A (F-15B-4) 71-291, a two-seat, advanced trainer in American Bicentennial colours. The first TF-15A, later redesignated F-15B, made its maiden flight on 7 July 1973. (*McDonnell Douglas*)

In May–June 1976, 20 Northrop F-5E Tiger II fighters arrived at Alconbury (01548 is pictured) where the 527th Tactical Fighter Aggressor Squadron was assigned to the 10th TRW, to help train the command's crews in air-to-air combat. (F-5E Tiger IIs also served in the Aggressor role at the 'Top Gun' US Navy Fighter Weapons School at NAS Miramar, California.) The F-5E Tiger II was the winner of the International Fighter Aircraft (IFA) competition on 20 November 1970 and the upgraded F-5E flew for the first time on 11 August 1972. The first Tiger IIs for the USAF were issued to the 425th Tactical Fighter Training Squadron at Chandler AFB, Arizona, on 4 April 1973. The 527th Tactical Fighter Aggressor Squadron was inactivated on 30 September 1990 at RAF Alconbury. (*USAFE*)

Northrop F-5E Tiger IIs have, like the F-5 Freedom Fighter before it, served many overseas air forces. The Tiger II has also been licence-built, by Canadair (for the indigenous armed forces and export), by CASA of Spain, as well as in South Korea and Taiwan. It has also been licence-built in Switzerland, where F-5Es were manufactured by the Federal Aircraft Factory for the Swiss Air Force (pictured). (*Author*)

Above: The General Dynamics YF-16 resulted from the 1972 competition for a lightweight air combat fighter (LWF) for the USAF. Two YF-16s were followed by six YF-16As (75-0748 is pictured), the first flying on 8 December 1976. The first full production F-16A flew in August 1978 and the 388th TFW at Hill AFB began to receive F16As and F-16Bs in January 1979. (*General Dynamics*)

Right: Left side air-to-air view of a Tactical Air Command F-15A Eagle 76-119 firing an AIM-7 Sparrow missile. (*USAF via Peter C. Smith*)

The F-14A Tomcat – the last naval aircraft in the famous Grumman cat family – was a result of an early 1960s USN requirement for a high-performance fighter to replace the aging F-4 Phantom. The first of twelve research and development aircraft made its maiden flight on 21 December 1970 and the first production aircraft was delivered to the Navy in June 1972. VF-1 'Wolf-pack' and VF-2 'Bounty Hunters' (F-14A of VF-2 is pictured) were established at Miramar, California, on 14 October 1972, and received their first Tomcats on 1 July 1973. When the Tomcat began an eight-month deployment to the Western Pacific with VF-1 and VF-2 onboard the 90,000-ton, nuclear-powered USS *Enterprise* (CVN-65) in mid-September 1974, it was the world's first operational air-superiority fighter with a variable-sweep wing. VF-1 and VF-2 moved to the USS *Ranger* (CV-61) in September 1980. They joined CVW-2, cruising onboard *Kitty Hawk* in early 1984, before returning to USS *Ranger*. (*Grumman*)

The first Atlantic fleet units equipped with the F-14A Tomcat were VF-14's 'Tophatters' and VF-32's 'Swordsmen' (pictured overflying the USS *John F Kennedy*) onboard the USS *John F Kennedy* (CV-67) in June 1975, to take up station with the 6th Fleet in the Mediterranean. (*Grumman*)

McDonnell RF-4C 66-0466 of the 179th Fighter Interceptor Squadron, Minnesota ANG, which began receiving RF-4Cs in place of F-101B/Fs in the winter of 1975. On 10 January 1976 this unit was redesignated the 179th TRS. In 1983–84 the 179th TRS traded its RF-4Cs for F-4D Phantoms. (*CONAM*)

In spring 1978 the 171st Fighter Interception Squadron, Michigan ANG, converted from F-106A/Bs to the F-4C Phantom (63-7595 is pictured). These were retained until July 1986 when Michigan ANG converted to the F-4D. (*CONAM*)

Right: F-14A Tomcats of VF-84 'Jolly Rogers', based on the USS *Nimitz*. 'Fighting 84' is the latest squadron to inherit VF-17's famous 'Jolly Rogers' skull and crossbones. (*Grumman*)

Below: Some 80 F-14As were accepted by the USN on behalf of the Imperial Iranian Air Force (IIAF) between December 1975 and July 1978. After the Shah was deposed in January 1979 the IIAF Tomcats were progressively cannibalised and others were lost in the long war against Iraq. (*Grumman*)

The BAe (formerly Hawker Siddeley) Sea Harrier FRS.I (fighter reconnaissance and strike) V/STOL aircraft for through-deck carriers of the Royal Navy was first flown on 20 August 1978. Changes from the RAF Harrier GR Mk 3, from which it was developed, included installation of Ferranti Blue Fox multi-mode radar in a re-styled nose, larger electronic HUD, passive ESW and radar warning receiver, removal of magnesium components and a raised cockpit. XZ450 (pictured), the first production example, made the first Sea Harrier landing on a carrier (HMS *Hermes*) on 14 November 1978. Deliveries to the Royal Navy for operation from *Invincible* class aircraft carriers equipped with 'ski-jumps' to allow higher-weight short take-offs, began on 18 June 1979, to RNAS Yeovilton (HMS *Heron*). (*BAe*)

The McDonnell Douglas F/A-18 Hornet was conceived as a multi-mission aircraft to supercede the F-4 Phantom fighter, A-4 Skyhawk and A-7E attack aircraft in USMC and USN squadrons. Pictured is the prototype (BuNo160775), which was rolled out at St Louis on 13 September 1978, and first flew on 18 November. Hornets first went to sea in February 1985 with VFA-25 (Strike-Fighter) 'Fist of the Fleet' and VFA-113 'Stingers', part of CVW-14 aboard the *Constellation* (CV-64). Altogether, 380 F/A-18A Hornets have been built for the USN and USMC. (*McDonnell Douglas*)

F-14A Tomcat of VF-51 'Screaming
Eagles'. (*Grumman*)